CENTRAL AUSTRALIA
Through the lens

Trevern and Anna Dawes

GOLDEN PRESS
Sydney   Auckland

Contents

Page

6   Introduction

22   The MacDonnell Ranges

38   The Olgas

52   Ayers Rock

68   Alice Springs

74   The Devils Marbles

80   Henbury Meteorite Craters National Park

84   Chambers Pillar

92   Gosse Bluff

98   Hermansburg Mission and Palm Valley

106   Kings Canyon

116   Mount Conner

122   Rainbow Valley

Scattered midday cloud casts shadow and sunlight patterns over the Olga domes.

Introduction

Introduction

The 'red centre' of Australia is one of the world's most ancient and splendid landscapes, a desert abounding in exotic natural features: stark, totem-like rocks, abrupt mountain ranges, dramatic gorges, and tranquil waterholes. Yet, despite the aridity and harshness, there exist a paradoxical fecundity and a remarkable collection of flora and fauna, including plants from pre-historic times and unique and strange animals.

The anomalous geology of Central Australia results from massive sinking and lifting of the land and continuous erosion by heat, cold, wind, and water. Mountains like the MacDonnell Ranges were formed in Pre-Cambrian times, when layers of quartzite, sandstone, shale, and limestone were pressured by earth movements into a series of parallel ranges rising to almost 3000 metres. Erosion gradually lowered the peaks and water sliced through the ridges to create gorges and clefts. Ormiston is the largest of these gorges and Standley Chasm the most unusual.

The region continues to be modified by weathering processes, in particular the erosive process known as exfoliation in which the large diurnal temperature range causes rock surfaces to expand and contract, resulting in the shedding, or peeling off, of surface material. Wind and water then soften sharp edges and, as moisture penetrates less-resistant rock layers, a chemical reaction may occur which, combined with the abrasive action of wind-blown sand particles, can sculpture caves or caverns. The granite blocks of the Devils Marbles are striking examples of exfoliation and, on a much larger scale, so are the rounded domes of the Olgas. The best-known cave formations are found around the base of Ayers Rock.

About 45 million years ago the continent of Australia broke away from Gondwanaland and began moving northward. As it entered warmer climes, inland lakes evaporated, rivers ceased to flow, lush vegetation disappeared, and winds shaped a landscape of sand dunes. Only in a few isolated places, such as Palm Valley, did ancient plant species manage to survive. Iron particles in the desert sand have produced a predominantly red and barren-looking landscape, but when good rains do fall dormant plant seeds are stimulated, streams flow, and the countryside assumes a brief but luscious spread of green.

When the sea level fell by about 75 metres during the last Ice Age, the inhabitants of Asia were able to venture into North America via the Bering Strait and down into Australia via Indonesia and New Guinea. Australia's first inhabitants were probably Negritos, south-east Asians seldom taller than 1.5 metres. They were followed by a succession of peoples, including the ancestors of today's Aborigines, before the land bridges were severed and the shallows inundated by melting ice.

Above: Standley Chasm, pictured here from the northern side, is one of the major tourist attractions in the West MacDonnell Ranges.

Previous page: Infrequent rainwater adds another dimension to the remarkable Kings Canyon landscape.

Top: Three huge domes on the eastern side of the Olgas glow almost luminous red at daybreak.

Bottom: Part of the rugged beauty of Ormiston Gorge is reflected in a long stretch of water near the southern entrance.

Introduction

The Aborigines have lived in Australia for at least 40,000 years. In order to practise a nomadic life within well-defined tribal territories the Aborigines of Central Australia have adapted to their environment by conserving resources and pursuing strict codes of conduct. Their way of life has an intensely spiritual foundation. They believe that the world and man originated in the *Tjukurapa*, or Dreamtime, a mystical period when the land was flat, featureless and adrift in a twilight zone, awaiting the actions of Great Ancestors to bestow shape and create life. Every major landscape feature is endowed with legendary characters, perpetuated throughout the centuries in song, story, dance, or ritual. Sites where the Great Ancestors returned to their birthplaces are held sacred. The affinity the Aborigines have for their territory is best appreciated in the knowledge that they consider not that they own the land but that the land owns them.

Aboriginal art, vividly represented in such places as the caves of Ayers Rock, portrays Dreamtime legends and common aspects of life. Curiously, the petroglyphs and stone arrangements to be found in Central Australia have little significance for the Aborigines other than that they are believed to be the work of Dreamtime spirits long before the advent of man.

The prospect of discovering a large inland sea and fertile land in the middle of Australia had captured the imagination of adventurous individuals ever since the first European settlement was established in Sydney in 1788. Captain Charles Sturt was the first to undertake a journey into Central Australia. On his 1844 expedition, his men endured terrible drought and stumbled across the stony surface of Sturt's Desert only to be turned back by the vast red sands of the Simpson Desert, about 650 kilometres from Australia's geographic centre. Ludwig Leichhardt, leading a party of six, made an attempt from Queensland in 1848. All members of the party disappeared without trace and are presumed to have perished in the Simpson Desert.

The South Australian Government, anxious to construct a telegraph link between Adelaide and Darwin, offered a £2000 bounty for the first expedition to make a crossing. John McDouall Stuart, a determined Scot and experienced explorer, took up the challenge. His expedition made rapid progress from Adelaide and after only seven weeks he reached the geographic centre, on 22 April 1860. En route he discovered the Finke River and Chambers Pillar, and passed through the West MacDonnell Ranges near Brinkleys Bluff. About 70 kilometres north of Tennant Creek, at a place now known as Attack Creek, the expedition was ambushed by Aborigines. Discouraged by the attack and suffering poor health, the party retreated. Back in Adelaide three months later, Stuart learned that an expedition sponsored by the

Top: There are many precariously balanced boulders to be found in the Devil's Marbles Conservation Reserve.

Bottom: Ewaninga Rock Carvings Conservation Reserve, located 90 kilometres south of Alice Springs, is one of several Central Australian sites where ancient petroglyphs are protected.

Top: Sheltered caves around the base of Ayers Rock contain Aboriginal paintings which symbolically depict legends of the Dreamtime.

Bottom: Some of the best preserved Aboriginal paintings in the MacDonnell Ranges are situated in Emily Gap.

Introduction

Royal Society of Victoria and led by Robert O'Hara Burke and William Wills had set off from Melbourne.

Still confident of beating Burke and Wills to the northern coast, Stuart left Adelaide a second time but once again was defeated, this time by thick scrub about 200 kilometres north of Attack Creek. Back in Adelaide, Stuart heard the news that the Burke and Wills expedition had been lost. Unperturbed by both this news and his own failures, Stuart decided to make a third and final attempt. On 24 July 1962 he reached Chambers Bay, 50 kilometres north-east of Darwin. He and his men barely survived the return journey and arrived in Adelaide to learn that, although Burke and Wills had died, their party had reached the Gulf of Carpentaria on 11 February 1862.

If John McDouall Stuart failed in his efforts to make the first north-south crossing of Australia he at least had the satisfaction of reaching the geographic centre and locating a practical route for the telegraph. His explorations were also instrumental in assisting the South Australian Government to gain control of the Northern Territory in 1863.

Ernest Giles, attempting to reach the west coast of Australia in his 1872 and 1873 expeditions, was not able to penetrate the western deserts but did discover Gosse Bluff, good grazing country along the George Gil Ranges and Palmer River, and was the first European to sight Ayers Rock and the Olgas. South Australia's Surveyor-General, William Christie Gosse, made a similar attempt to reach the west coast in 1873. Although also repelled by desert, he at least claimed the notable honour of being the first explorer to reach Ayers Rock and the Olgas.

The average annual rainfall in Central Australia is less than 250 millimetres; this rainfall is erratic, the annual evaporation rate exceeds 2500 millimetres, and summer temperatures can hover for many days above 40°C (Alice Springs recorded 46.7°C in 1883) and fall to below freezing point on winter nights. In such a forbidding environment water is a key factor and, in spite of its scarcity, over 1000 plant species have been recorded.

Native flora is grouped into three broad categories: colourful, quick-growing, short-lived plants such as wildflowers; semi-deciduous trees and shrubs which have the capacity to drop their leaves in drought conditions; and perennials with deep-root storage systems. Drought-resistant spinifex grassland and mulga scrub form the dominant vegetation of the region. The much maligned spinifex plays an important role in desert ecology; it not only provides food, shade, and protection for small animals but also prevents erosion by binding sand together.

Ghost gums, made famous by Albert Namatjira and other artists, are imposing trees, as are river red gums, whose extensive root systems reach permanent water along

Top: Central Australia is famous for its tree lined gorges and sheltered rock pools.

Bottom: Needle sharp spinifex, pictured here in Gosse Bluff, makes optimum use of meagre rainfall and has the ability to reduce water loss during drought.

Previous page: Verdant spinifex spreads to the horizon along the road to Arltunga.

Top: Palm Valley supports about 300 species of plants, including the rare cabbage palm "Livistonia Mariae".

Bottom: There are numerous species of Mulla Mulla, the dry region plant with the fluffy flowerhead, to be seen in the Central Australian springtime.

Top: Eucalyptus flowers are a mass of delicate stamens unsupported by petals.

Bottom: The attractive pink everlasting "paper daisy" is a small annual which generally prefers red sandy soils.

15

creek beds and around waterholes. In the midst of this desert landscape are several unlikely plant species with origins dating back to prehistoric times. The most notable are cabbage palms, found in Palm Valley and other tributaries of the Finke River, and cycads in the MacDonnell Ranges.

Desert-survival systems have been developed by animals, too, many species being able to retain moisture in their bodies for lengthy periods. Frogs, for example, are virtually self-contained waterbottles, existing in a dormant state in cool, underground tunnels until adequate rains fall. The larger marsupials, the kangaroo, euro and wallaby, are shy and elusive and rarely seen along tourist routes. Fortunately, there are exceptions like the almost-tame colony of black-flanked rock wallabies at Simpsons Gap. The red kangaroo grows to 2 metres and may attain a weight of 100 kilograms; the robust euro is extremely timid and prefers to keep to rock terrain; small marsupials such as the red-eared antechinus and the mole are usually located only by patient naturalists.

One of Central Australia's best known animals is the dingo. This wild dog came to Australia with the Aborigines and is now classified as native fauna. Basically individualistic, intelligent, and relatively common, the dingo assumes a special role in the ecology of Central Australia, if not of the entire continent. It is often blamed for damage caused by feral dogs and, as such, may be regarded as a threat to livestock, but it does maintain a vital check on the rabbit population.

The presence of man and the release of domestic animals into the environment (camels, donkeys, rabbits, cats, and dogs) has had an unfavourable effect on the natural habitat. Several native species are now thought to be extinct and others are already classified as endangered.

Central Australia has an impressive collection of reptiles but they are essentially nocturnal, wary of man and, consequently, difficult to observe. Being cold-blooded creatures, their body temperatures are dependent on the environment. The smaller lizards like the gecko warm up quickly whereas the larger bearded dragon has the ability to spread its body to absorb ground heat. Notable among the lizards are the fierce-looking yet harmless ant-eating thorny devil and the giant perentie. Growing to a length of 2 metres, the perentie has the distinction of being the world's second-largest lizard, surpassed only by the komodo dragon of Indonesia.

The western brown and king brown are the largest of the poisonous snakes. Potentially dangerous as they may be, these and other snakes will avoid man at every opportunity. The children's python is a large and most attractive snake which, as its name implies is gentle and harmless.

The birds of Central Australia number about 200

Top: Despite its grotesque appearance the Thorny Devil is a harmless reptile which lives on a diet of small ants.

Bottom: Black Flanked Rock Wallabies, normally elusive and timid creatures, have grown accustomed to people in Simpson's Gap. They may be seen at close range, especially when called by the Park Rangers for feeding.

Top: Bearded Dragons are a relatively common reptile in Central Australia. They enjoy basking in the sun and rely heavily on camouflage and absolute stillness for protection. When threatened they readily adopt a defensive stance and expand their beards to increase their presence.

Bottom: Herds of wild donkeys find the terrain of the MacDonnell Ranges to their liking but their numbers are a threat to native flora and fauna.

Introduction

species. Many have the ability to acquire moisture from small animals and dew, and so are not entirely reliant on permanent waterholes. The best-known birds are the emu, galah, parrot, cockatoo, budgerigar, bustard, wedge-tailed eagle.

Ayers Rock, the world's largest monolith, is without doubt the highlight of Central Australia. To see it is to believe it and the climb to the top is an exhilarating achievement. But 'the rock' is only part of the Central Australian adventure. Add the mystique of the Olgas, the serenity of gorges like Ormiston, the attractions of 'the Alice', and all the other inevitable surprises: Australia's red centre becomes an experience that rarely fails to leave an impression.

Top: Misty rain swirling around the Dome of the Dying Kangaroo Man adds to the mystique of one of the strange formations of the Olgas.

Bottom: The head of Kings Canyon provides a cool retreat after a rugged hike along Kings Creek.

Previous page: The Finke River and Glen Helen Gorge viewed from a ridge on the western bank.

20

Top: As the annual rainfall in Central Australia is very low it is an unusual occurrence to see the surface of Ayers Rock wet and grey.

Bottom: Many attractive areas in Central Australia, like the gorge above Kathleen Spring in the George Gill Range, are seldom seen by organised tour groups.

The MacDonnell Ranges

The MacDonnell Ranges

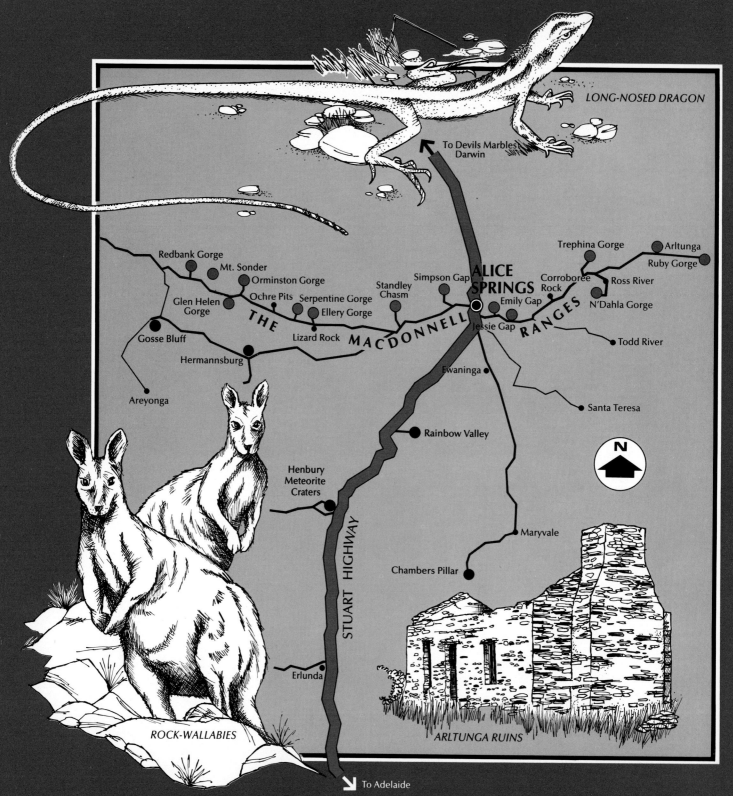

LONG-NOSED DRAGON

To Devils Marbles
Darwin

Redbank Gorge

Mt. Sonder

Orminston Gorge

Glen Helen
Gorge

Ochre Pits

Serpentine Gorge

Ellery Gorge

Lizard Rock

Standley
Chasm

Simpson Gap

ALICE
SPRINGS

Emily Gap

Jessie Gap

Trephina Gorge

Arltunga

Ruby Gorge

Corroboree
Rock

Ross River

N'Dahla Gorge

Todd River

THE MACDONNELL RANGES

Gosse Bluff

Hermannsburg

Areyonga

Ewaninga

Santa Teresa

Rainbow Valley

Henbury
Meteorite
Craters

STUART HIGHWAY

Maryvale

Chambers Pillar

Erlunda

To Adelaide

N

ROCK-WALLABIES

ARLTUNGA RUINS

Previous page: Soft, late afternoon light brings a picturesque quality to the West MacDonnell Ranges.

Facing page: The track to N'Dhala Gorge in the East MacDonnell Ranges crosses Ross River several times and parallels spectacular walls of fractured rock.

The MacDonnell Ranges

The MacDonnell Ranges, a series of parallel ridges running in an east-west direction for nearly 500 kilometres, occupy almost the precise geographic centre of Australia. Although they do not attain great heights they are nonetheless spectacular: the mountains rise abruptly, are cut by many gorges, and are noted for their clarity of form and colour. This is *Altjira,* the eternal land, ancient and serene.

The MacDonnells are mere remnants of a much larger range deposited between 1400 and 2000 million years ago. About 1000 million years ago extreme folding elevated the rocks to form the MacDonnell Ranges and the adjacent Chewing and Hart ranges. At that time the mountains rose to about 3000 metres. Erosion removed sediments which were deposited in seas, and about 500 million years ago these young sediments were uplifted and folded to become the George Gil, Krichauff and Waterhouse ranges.

Today the MacDonnell Ranges stand about 600 metres above sea level and have an average height of 400-500 metres. They consist primarily of quartzite and are stained with iron oxide. The more resistant rock forms the prominent peaks, including Mount Heughlin (1450 metres above sea level), Mount Edward (1418 metres) Mount Sonder (1334 metres), and Mount Hay (1249 metres).

The main attractions of the MacDonnell Ranges are the gorges. Most of them contain permanent water and support a variety of flora and fauna; some of the waterholes are surprisingly deep and the water is very cold. The low water temperature is attributed to depth and the fact that sunlight only strikes the surface for a brief period each day. Scattered around the waterholes and along dry creek beds are fine specimens of bloodwood, corkwood, ironbark, and majestic river red and ghost gums. Cycads, rare plants with a 200-million-year history, may be found in well-shaded areas.

John McDouall Stuart and two companions, reached the ranges from the south on 12 April 1860 and named them after Sir Richard MacDonnell, then Governor of South Australia. The pastoral potential of the area impressed Stuart but he was anxious to reach the north coast of Australia and so failed to explore the ranges in detail.

The establishment of the Overland Telegraph Line in 1870-72 and the construction of the repeater station at Alice Springs heralded the beginnings of permanent European settlement in the MacDonnells. Ernest Giles and William Christie Gosse made separate journeys to the western end of the ranges in 1872-73 and Peter Egerton Warburton followed the same direction in his 1873 expedition to the west coast of Australia. The East MacDonnells were explored by David Lindsay in 1885, gold discovered at Arltunga in 1887.

Above: Although not the highest peak in the West MacDonnell Ranges Mt. Sonder is a dominant landmark and a favourite subject for painters and photographers.

West MacDonnell Ranges

The sealed surface of Larapinta Drive connects all the well-known sites, national parks and reserves of the West MacDonnell Ranges. From Alice Springs it is a short drive to John Flynn's Grave Historic Reserve, Honeymoon Gap, the famous twin ghost gums, and Simpsons Gap National Park. Artist Albert Namatjira's scene depicting twin ghost gums against a background of dramatic mountains is one of the great photographic clichés of Central Australia. However it is a wonderful sight and there are many other splendid tree and mountain picture combinations in the area.

Simpsons Gap National Park, previously part of a pastoral lease, was dedicated in 1958 and now occupies 30950 hectares. It is part of the Runatjirba Ridge and, according to the Aranda Aborigines, is the home of the Giant Goanna Ancestors, or Big Lizard People.

Gilbert McMinn, a member of the Overland Telegraph survey party, discovered Simpsons Gap on 22 February 1871. The naming of the gap remains a mystery, but it seems certain that it bears no link with the Simpson Desert. The dry creek bed passing through the gap is a tributary of the Todd River and has been successively known as Simpson, Temple Bar and Roe Creek.

The Park has several good walks, one of the most popular being the half-kilometre stroll to Cassia Hill for a distant view of the gap and panoramas of the surrounding countryside. Apart from the beauty of the Simpsons Gap, its stately gums and brilliant white sands, there is the attraction of black-flanked rock wallabies. These timid animals are fed daily by rangers and can therefore be observed at close quarters.

Standley Chasm lies 50 kilometres west of Alice Springs and is probably the best-known landmark in the MacDonnell Ranges. This spectacular 9-metre-wide cleft in the Chewing Range is 70 metres high and only at midday does the sun illuminate the chasm and reveal the colour of the rich quartzite rocks. The area was originally called Galls Spring (although technically not a spring) after Charles Gall, the second manager of Owen Spring Station, but was renamed Standley Chasm after Mrs Ida Standley, the first school teacher in Alice Springs and the first white woman to walk through the cleft. The chasm is part of Jay Creek Aboriginal Reserve. It is so popular that it is virtually impossible to enjoy alone the midday play of light.

Ellery Creek Big Hole Reserve, known by the Aborigines as *Udepta*, is 90 kilometres from Alice Springs and covers an area of 1766 hectares. Picturesque trees, sandy shores and cool, reflective waters bring a charming tranquility to the waterhole, the northern side of which can be reached by paddling across on an airbed, one of the centre's favourite 'water craft'. Ellery Creek was discovered by Ernest Giles in 1872 and was named after

Top: The abrupt eastern entrance to Ormiston Gorge viewed from Ormiston Pound.

Bottom: Simpsons Gap, pictured from Cassia Hill, is situated in the Runatjirba Ridge section of the West MacDonnell Ranges, 8 kilometres west of Alice Springs.

Top: One of the Devil's Marbles' granite boulders, weighing eight tonnes, marks the grave site at the base of Mt. Gillen of Reverend John Flynn, the bush padre who established the Flying Doctor Service and the Australian Inland Mission.

Bottom: The stately twin ghost gums set against a mountain range were immortalised in a famous painting by Aboriginal artist Albert Namatjira. The site has since become an irresistible photo stop for visitors travelling into the West MacDonnell Ranges.

R.L.J. Ellery, government astronomer and director of the Melbourne Observatory. The name 'Big Hole' was used by local stockmen to distinguish it from other Ellery Creek waterholes.

Serpentine Gorge Reserve occupies only 500 hectares and is located 7 kilometres to the west of Ellery Creek. The gorge is wide and colourful but the southern entrance is usually blocked by a waterhole and only those willing to swim in the chilly water or paddle across in a boat or on an airbed can enjoy its features. The climb up over the range and into the gorge is an arduous one.

Ormiston Gorge lies 132 kilometres from Alice Springs and was named by Colonel P.E. Warburton in 1873. Enclosed by steep walls as high as 250 metres, its grandeur and colour have earnt it the title of 'jewel of the centre'. The gorge contains several large waterholes and some curious aspects, such as gum trees clinging to unlikely footholds high up in the rocks. Few visitors venture far into Ormiston Gorge and therefore miss out on some superb scenery and the chance to see the gorge opening out into the Pound. This broad area is about 10 kilometres in diameter and has the prominent peak of Mount Giles on the eastern side. The gorge was used for watering cattle until the creation of the 4655 hectare Ormiston Gorge and Pound National Park. Water pollution, erosion and the destruction of vegetation have since been controlled and the gorge has reverted to its natural state.

Ormiston Creek flows south through the gorge and eventually joins the Finke River and Glen Helen Gorge. This wide gorge, discovered on 6 September 1872 by Ernest Giles, contains a large waterhole. The aborigines know the waterhole as *Japala* and believe it to be the site where the first shapeless Dreamtime beings originated. The naming of Glen Helen is attributed to several sources, with that of Frederick Raggatt being the most favoured. He assumed control of a pastoral lease in the area at the turn of the century and is believed to have named the gorge after his niece Helen Wakefield. The Glen Helen Nature Park (386 hectares) includes the actual gorge but not Glen Helen chalet, the original home of Raggatt.

Further west, across the Finke River, lies Mount Sonder. At 1334 metres above sea level it is not the highest peak in the West MacDonnell Ranges but it is very prominent and a favourite subject for painters and photographers. Mount Sonder was named by Ferdinand von Mueller after Dr William Sonder of Adelaide, and is known to the Aborigines as *Rutjipma*.

Redbank Gorge Nature Park, a relatively isolated area of 1295 hectares, lies 30 kilometres to the west of Glen Helen. A 1-kilometre walk over sand and rocks is necessary to reach the spectacular gorge. The northern side of Redbank Gorge, like Ellery Creek Big Hole and Serpentine Gorge, can only be reached by water.

Above: During the peak tourist season many visitors gather in Standley Chasm to watch the midday play of light on the orange quartzite walls.

Top: Ellery Creek Big Hole Reserve, situated 90
kilometres west of Alice Springs, is a pleasant place to
spend a relaxing few hours. The water is deep and
surprisingly cold, even in the middle of summer.

Bottom: There are several dramatic quartzite formations
to be found in Glen Helen Gorge.

East MacDonnell Ranges

Emily and Jessie Gap reserves have an area of 695 hectares and are only 15 minutes' drive from Alice Springs. Emily Gap is unspectacular but attractive and contains some interesting Aboriginal paintings. By comparison, Jessie Gap is little more than a break in a low section of the range. Both gorges were named after the wives of early surveyors and were permanent Aboriginal waterholes until 1975, when flooding filled them with sand.

Some 40 kilometres to the east of Alice Springs lies the 7-hectare Corroboree Rock Scenic Reserve, with its single outcrop of vertical dolomite strata and horizontal joint planes. The hole through the rock, caused by the loss of a joint block, is said to have been a storehouse for sacred implements *(tjuringa)* belonging to the Aranda tribe.

Located 70 kilometres from Alice Springs, Trephina Gorge Nature Park (1770 hectares) contains both the impressive red-walled Trephina Gorge and the John Hayes waterhole. The names are attributed to Trephina Benstead and John Hayes, early pioneers who helped establish pastoral lands in the district. The gorge has a broad, sandy creek bed, with waterholes that linger well after rain, and some beautiful river red gums. The fractured rock shelves and crevices provide shelter for numerous reptiles, including the tiny military dragon and the perentie. Excellent views of the surrounding ranges may be gained by climbing to the top of the gorge. John Hayes waterhole, part of an area known as the Valley of the Eagles, is an intimate place enclosed by steep walls. A single river red gum stands by the edge of the main pool while figs and ferns cling to the rock walls.

The road to Ross River Homestead and N'Dhala Gorge Scenic Reserve lies a few kilometres past the turn-off to Trephina Gorge. At N'Dhala, petroglyphs estimated to be some 20000 years old are of interest.

All these features in the East MacDonnell Ranges can be comfortably viewed in a day's outing from Alice Springs. Camping gear and, preferably, a four-wheel-drive vehicle are necessary for those wishing to penetrate further east to Arltunga and Ruby Gorge.

Arltunga Goldfield Reserve (4893 hectares) is situated just over 100 kilometres from Alice Springs. The reserve protects remnants from the gold-mining era, at the turn of the century. Joseph Hele and Isaac Smith discovered alluvial gold in April 1887 along a dry creek bed downstream from Paddys Rockhole. Ten years later, reef gold was found by H.E. Luce on White Range, a few kilometres to the east.

Conditions were harsh on the goldfields. The problems of heat, dust, scarcity of water, and lack of medical facilities meant only the hardiest and the lucky would remain. Today, the remnants of houses built from slabs of weathered rock, the cyanide works, police

Top: A small area west of Serpentine Gorge, known as the Ochre Pits, has colourful strata layers which were a prime source of material for traditional Aboriginal paintings.

Bottom: Emily Gap, a convenient 10 kilometre drive east of Alice Springs, is a favourite picnic spot for both tourists and locals.

Top: Erosive forces have sculptured some weird shapes n rock outcrops of the West MacDonnell Ranges. The istinctive formation of Lizard Rock may be seen along he Larapinta Drive roadside.

Bottom: The broad, sandy creekbed of Trephina Gorge s lined with river red gums and contains several deep waterholes and stark rock faces.

station, and rusted machinery are stark monuments to men who were prepared to sacrifice every comfort in an effort to extract some wealth from an arid land.

The route to Ruby Gorge demands the use of a four-wheel-drive vehicle and considerable care in negotiating treacherous sand. This is the place where explorer David Lindsay discovered bright red gems in March 1886, however, what were initially considered to be rubies proved to be only garnets. The gorge, 40 kilometres from Arltunga and approached by a track deviating northwards from the Atnarpa Homestead windmill and water tanks, has retained its inappropriate name.

Above: Corroboree Rock is an imposing dolomite dyke in the East MacDonnell Ranges. The Arunta Aboriginals know it as Antanangantana, the place where sacred tribal objects were once stored.

Top: Dancing Lubra Rock is a series of parallel fault outcrops located between N'Dhala Gorge and Ross River Homestead.

Bottom left: N'Dhala Gorge is not only noted for its unusual rock carvings but also for steep walls and abrupt ramparts.

Bottom right: John Hayes waterhole is part of Trephina Gorge Nature Park. There are two waterholes, an outer one pictured here and a secluded inner one enclosed by high rock walls.

Top: Arltunga is the Aboriginal place name for Paddy's Rockhole, the area where alluvial, and later reef gold was mined following a discovery by Joseph Hele in 1887. A handful of stone buildings, mining equipment and the inevitable graves are stark monuments of a harsh era.

Bottom left: The tranquil atmosphere of Ruby Gorge, located about 40 kilometres east of Arltunga, suggests none of the frenzy associated with the ''ruby rush'' of the late 1880s.

Bottom right: The ancient petroglyphs in N'Dhala Gorge, which appear to depict headdressed figures, are considered to be amongst the earliest ritual markings of mankind.

The Olgas

The Olgas

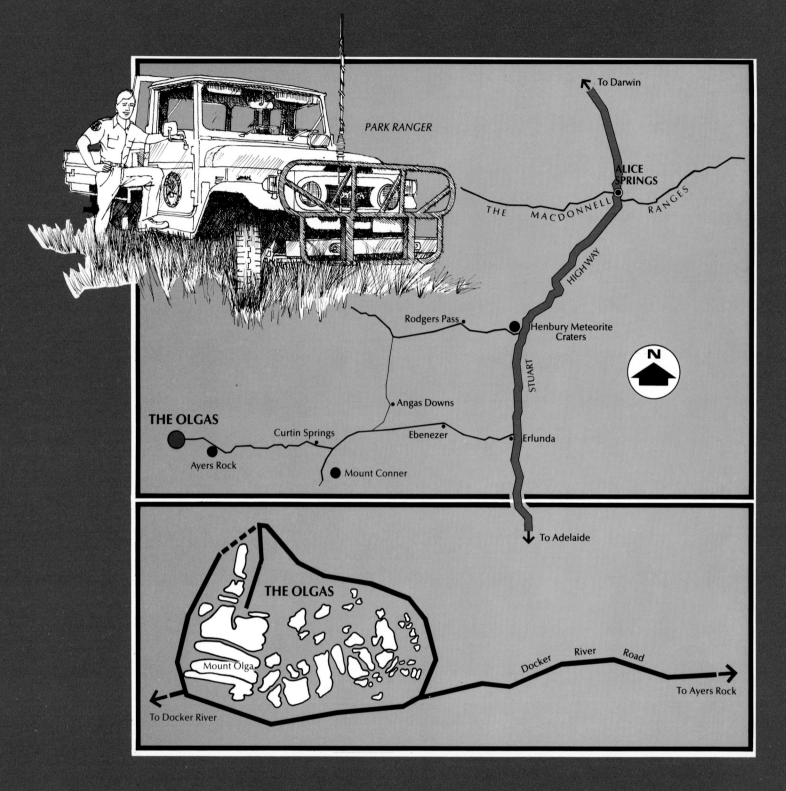

PARK RANGER

To Darwin

ALICE SPRINGS

THE MACDONNELL RANGES

Rodgers Pass

Henbury Meteorite Craters

HIGHWAY

STUART

N

Angas Downs

THE OLGAS

Curtin Springs

Ebenezer

Erlunda

Ayers Rock

Mount Conner

To Adelaide

THE OLGAS

Mount Olga

Docker River Road

To Ayers Rock

To Docker River

Previous page: Filtered sunlight highlights the outline of the Olgas as viewed from sandhills on the eastern side.

Facing page: The walk to the Valley of the Winds follows a creek bed, skirts around the base of a towering dome and leads to an elevated ridge overlooking the vast valley and eastern domes of the Olgas.

The Olgas

'The appearance of Mount Olga from this camp is truly wonderful; it displayed to our astonished eyes, rounded minarets, giant cupolas and monstrous domes. There they have stood as huge memorials from the ancient times of earth, for ages, countless eons of ages since Creation first had birth. Time, the old, the dim magician, has ineffectually laboured here . . .'

Explorer Ernest Giles

The Olgas are located 32 kilometres to the west of Ayers Rock, and about 450 kilometres south-west of Alice Springs. They stretch east-west for about 9 kilometres and north-south for about 5 kilometres. The tallest of the 31 domes, Mount Olga, is 546 metres above the surrounding desert and 1072 metres above sea level. Many of the adjacent domes in the westen sector are almost as high and most are at least half as high again as Ayers Rock.

The story of the Olgas began about 600 million years ago when, geologists believe, one of the many seas that inundated the region tore material from ranges to the south-east. Fragments of granite, gneiss and volcanic rocks were rolled smooth, dumped in an encirclement, and finally cemented together with fine sand particles. About 500 million years ago the conglomerate was lifted above the sea, and the rock strata tilted about 20 degrees to the horizontal. Over millions of years erosion has lowered the level of the plain and left, hard resilient rock. But, whereas Ayers Rock remained as one solid piece, the Olgas have evolved into a grouping of independent structures.

They consist of two sets of vertical joint planes at right angles to each other. Individual joints are widely spaced. As weathering occurred these spaces were etched, leaving huge blocks of rock. The principal erosive force was off-loading, a process in which internal rock pressures are released, causing large slabs to break away in cracks parallel to the ground. These slabs weathered into boulders which either fell into the gorges and valleys or were left to balance precariously. The dome tops have rounded and their sides have become steeper with the continuing off-loading process. The distinct 'pudding stone' conglomerate of the Olgas has eroded evenly because of the similarity in rock hardness. In some places the surface resembles a complex mosaic. Additonal patterns have formed on shaded walls, and green, red and orange lichens combine with black algae stains. The most prominent patterns exist on the southern face of Liru Mountain.

European contact with the Olgas began just over a century ago, when Ayers Rock and the Olgas were sighted by a small party led by Ernest Giles. As he gazed towards the horizon, Giles was particularly impressed, not by Ayers Rock, but by the strange mountains that he had

Above: A wide-angle lens dramatically alters the perspective of one of the Kalajiri Rockholes on the track to the Valley of the Winds.

The Olgas

sighted. Unfortunately, the treacherous salt surface of a great lake impeded his progress and, after several attempts to cross the mud at the edge of the lake, he was forced to retreat eastwards via the George Gill Range to the Alice Springs-Adelaide telegraph line.

Giles would have preferred to name both distant mountain and lake after his patron, Baron Ferdinand von Mueller, but the distinguished botanist had recently been honoured with the Spanish Order of St Isabella and insisted that his name be overlooked. Lake Amadeus is therefore named after Amadeo, King of Spain, and Mount Olga after the Grand Duchess Olga Constantinova of Russia, wife of King George of the Hellenes. The Olgas has since become the convenient pluralised name for the entire complex of domes.

Determined to reach the Olgas, Giles organised a second expedition, but he was beaten by William Christie Gosse who arrived at Mount Olga on 8 August 1873. Gosse managed to scramble about 300 metres up the western side of Mount Olga before being discouraged from proceeding further by the difficulty of the descent. Giles arrived at the base of Mount Olga on 14 of September; he experienced elation and then bitter disappointment upon discovering tracks from the Gosse expedition. He, too, attempted to scale the mountain but was obliged to retire.

The early Aborigines, who had learned to adapt to their harsh environment and conserve its meagre resources, created many Olga Dreamtime legends. Unfortunately, accurate details of these legends and cultural life are now lost because the descendants of the original inhabitants have not survived. The surrounding tribes, the Yankuntjatjara and the Pitjantjatjara, have absorbed some remnants of the early legends into their own folklore.

The Aborigines know the Olgas as *Katatjuta*, meaning many heads, and claim that every major totemic feature and waterhole had its origin in the Dreamtime. For example, there is a legend about the dome of the Dying Kangaroo Man: he died in his sister's arms after being attacked by dingoes. An eroded cavity in a pillar represents his wound and the part of his body torn away is represented by a rock at the base of the mound.

The large domes on the western side of the Olgas are said to be bodies of the fearsome *pungalunga*, the giant cannibals who consumed only Aborigines. But perhaps the most popular legend concerns *Wanambi*, the enormous serpent who lives in a huge cave deep inside Mount Olga. When tribal indiscretions occur, Wanambi vents his anger with great gusts of wind through the gorges. When revenge is satisfied, he transforms himself into a rainbow across the domes.

Owing to the lack of smooth rock surfaces in well-sheltered positions there is only one known Aboriginal

Top: The Dome of the Dying Kangaroo Man stands several hundred metres high and is an unmistakeable feature on the southern side of the Olgas.

Bottom: A small waterfall in the Valley of the Winds is one of the pleasant surprises that may be found after rain.

Top: Katatjuta lookout has several vantage points overlooking the Olga domes and surrounding desert.

Bottom: The unusual vertical patterns on the side of Liru Mountain are a combination of green, red and orange lichens and black algae stains.

The Olgas

drawing and this is located on the western side of the Olga Gorge. There is, however, a small collection of petroglyphs around the Olga, Tuin and Wina waterholes. These are simple geometric designs, or impressions, of emu, heron, kangaroo, or wallaby tracks. The most common designs are concentric *tjuringa* circles. According to the Aborigines, these rock markings are not the work of their ancestors; rather, they are evidence of an ancient art practised by the mythological people who inhabited the area well before the Dreamtime.

There are also some stone arrangements, once again not attributable to recent Aboriginal forebears but more likely to be the work of the first Aborigines to journey south through the region. Significantly, these sites are usually close to waterholes or soaks. Some have been disturbed by animals or, sadly, by people unaware of the importance of the formations.

A rough vehicular track of some 30 kilometres encircles the Olgas, providing access to Olga Gorge, a sunset-viewing area, the Katatjuta lookout, and the Valley of the Winds. The north-western section of the track is rough and has a four-wheel-drive rating.

Only a few domes can be easily climbed. Most are almost vertical and surfaces are fragile. From a distance, Mount Olga appears insurmountable, but it can nonetheless be scaled freehand by experienced rock climbers. Compared to the many thousands who climb Ayers Rock every year, only a few dozen manage to reach the top of Mount Olga. Climbers are, of course, expected to register their intention with the rangers.

Despite the low rainfall and the lack of permanent waterholes, shaded areas can retain moisture for long periods. This moisture, and lingering waterholes, support a great variety of wildlife. Birds are abundant: goshawks and wedge-tailed eagles soaring high above; the bewitching calls of Port Lincoln parrots and pied butcher-birds can often be heard. Other prominent birds are western bowerbirds, grey-headed honeyeaters, willie wagtails, red-backed kingfishers, crested bellbirds, tawny frogmouths, zebra finches and budgerigars. In favourable conditions, the finches and budgerigars are prolific breeders and when flocks fly close overhead the sound resembles a sudden gush of wind.

Western brown and yellow-tailed whip snakes, the two poisonous reptiles in the area, are rarely seen. Potentially dangerous as they may be, these reptiles are extremely shy and will avoid human contact wherever possible. Only when cornered or threatened will they assume an attacking posture.

The elusive euro (a rock-climbing kangaroo) finds a comfortable home in the Olgas but it, too, is rarely encountered at close range. The only creatures likely to stand their ground are small skinks and dragon lizards and

Top: The Aboriginals believe that the petroglyphs in the Olgas, and indeed throughout Central Australia, are not the work of man but were created by Dreamtime Spirit Ancestors.

Bottom: A series of caves, their floors strewn with rubble from collapsed ceilings, lie underneath a group of huge boulders in a remote part of the Olgas.

Above: A tranquil rockpool is an ideal mirror to reflect
the intense sunset colour on the towering walls of Olga
Gorge.

The Olgas

they usually do so out of curiosity. The greatest activity occurs at night. Dingoes compete with feral cats for small game, and all manner of insects are on the move.

Spring is by far the most pleasant time to visit the Olgas; the weather is agreeable and there is the likelihood of masses of wildflower colour. Carpets of yellow everlasting daisies and vast tracts of wild hops (ruby dock) are common around the perimeter of the domes, while the interior contains a remarkable diversity of wildflower species.

The Olgas are a semi-wilderness and, provided they do not suffer from 'visitor saturation', the enjoyment of the mystical domes and spectacular gorges as a purely personal encounter will remain untarnished. However, they are slowly gaining prominence in Central Australian tourist itineraries. Like Ernest Giles, many latter day explorers-at-heart will discover that the 'huge memorials of the ancient times of earth' do make a marvellous impression.

Top: Sturt's Desert Rose is the official floral emblem of the Northern Territory.

Bottom: Two of the Olga domes framed through a diffusion of wildflower colour.

Top: Vast tracts of Red Ruby Dock (wild hops) are a common sight during springtime along the road leading to the eastern side of the Olgas.

Bottom: A glint of sunlight catches a group of Mulla Mulla in the Valley of the Winds.

49

Facing Page: An aerial view permits a complete perspective of the Olga domes and there could be no more appropriate time to be flying than at sunset.

Top: Mt. Ghee, Mt. Walpa, Mt. Olga and Liru Mountain attain a purple silhouette in the early dawn.

Bottom: Many visitors to Uluru National Park consider the sunset sequence of the Olgas to be equally, if not more impressive, than that of Ayers Rock.

Ayers Rock

Ayers Rock

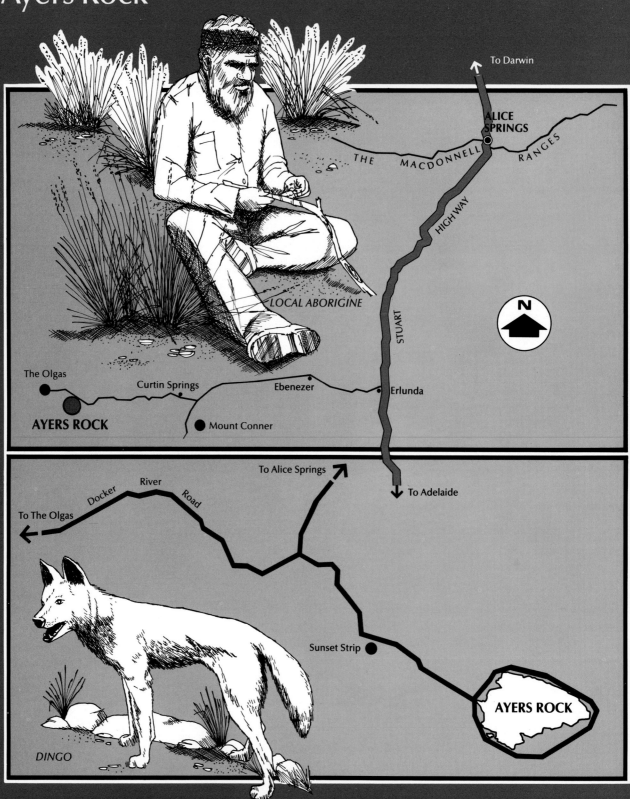

LOCAL ABORIGINE

To Darwin

ALICE SPRINGS

THE MACDONNELL RANGES

STUART HIGHWAY

N

The Olgas

Curtin Springs

Ebenezer

Erlunda

AYERS ROCK

Mount Conner

To Alice Springs

To Adelaide

Docker River Road

To The Olgas

Sunset Strip

AYERS ROCK

DINGO

Previous page: A desert oak frames Ayers Rock at sunrise as viewed from a ridge of sandhills overlooking the former camping grounds.

Facing page: The extraordinary landscape which forms on the top of Ayers Rock after a heavy downpour is shortlived as wind and sun quickly evaporate the series of small, shallow pools.

Ayers Rock

'Certainly the most wonderful natural feature I have ever seen ... this rock appears more wonderful every time I look at it, and I might say it is a sight worth riding over 84 miles of spinifex sandhills to see.'
Explorer William Christie Gosse

Ayers Rock or Uluru, lies 478 kilometres south-east of Alice Springs. Isolated in the midst of sandy plains, dunes and mulga scrubland, it is the world's largest monolith — an inselberg, or island mountain, penetrating some 6000 metres underground. The 'Cathedral of the Desert' is 348 metres above ground level and 867 metres above sea level; it is 3.6 kilometres long and 2.4 kilometres wide, and has a circumference of 8.8 kilometres.

During the Cambrian period, some 600 million years ago, mineral fragments were eroded from an ancient land mass and compressed into a highly resistant coarse sandstone called arkose. About 500 million years ago that arkose was uplifted and folded, causing a massive amount of rock to be tilted into an almost vertical position. Erosion then removed the less resistant layers and shaped the great monolith, a monolith that has remained essentially unchanged for some 40 million years.

The surface of Ayers Rock is subject to an extremely slow but continuous process called spalling, or exfoliation: expansion and contraction of the rock surface caused by temperature extremes and moisture, mostly in the form of dew, produce the flaky appearance characteristic of the Rock. As well, the moisture combines chemically with the air to produce iron oxides, and these give rise to its distinctive rusty colour. All the caves, both at ground level and elevated, have been formed by extensive exfoliation along weaker sandstone strata. Commencing from a mere dent in the surface, the process continues upwards and inwards to create wave-like shapes. Overhangs eventually collapse under their own weight and form piles of rock at the cave entrances. The best-known cave is a series of shallow hollows high on the northern face, called the Brain, or Ngoru (ritual chest scars).

Some features are the result of unloading, such as the 100-metre-high Ngaltawaddi (sacred digging stick), often incorrectly termed the Kangaroo Tail. This section of rock was subjected to enormous pressure whilst buried and when erosion removed, or unloaded, overlying rocks it expanded and formed a crack parallel to the main rock.

Of all the creatures associated with Ayers Rock the shield and fairy shrimps are among the most remarkable. These tiny animals inhabit pools on top of the rock and have the capacity to lay eggs which remain dormant in dry sand until rain occurs. The shield shrimp is believed to have existed on the rock for 150 million years.

Above: Ayers Rock is the world's largest monolith. Standing 348 metres above ground level and with a circumference of 8.8 kilometres the Rock has a commanding presence in the vast desert expanse.

Ayers Rock

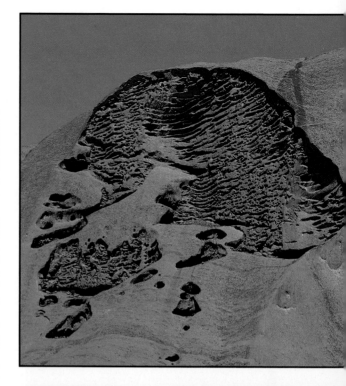

Although the average annual rainfall of 200 millimetres is small and the annual evaporation rate of 2750 millimetres is extremely high, the Ayers Rock watershed provides a moisture zone in the immediate area. This zone supports tree and scrub cover and a variety of wildlife, but native fauna such as kangaroos, dingoes, reptiles, and birds must now compete with feral cats, rabbits, foxes, camels and, in increasing numbers, man.

Ernest Giles was the first to sight and record both Ayers Rock and the Olgas. In October 1872 he gazed through smoke haze from the shores of Lake Amadeus, some 40 kilometres away. The treacherous surface of the salt lake impeded his progress and he was forced to retreat, leaving William Christie Gosse, the Deputy Surveyor-General of South Australia, to be the first white man to reach Ayers Rock.

Gosse, accompanied by an Afghan camel driver named Kamran, arrived at the rock on 19 July 1873, having followed a line of waterholes discovered by Ernest Giles. Surprised by the enormity of the 'hill' he sighted from afar, Gosse allocated to it the name Ayers Rock, after Sir Henry Ayers, then Premier of South Australia. The following day, Gosse and Kamran reached the summit by climbing barefooted up the steep valley above Maggie Springs.

William Harry Tietkins, formerly second-in-command on some of the Giles expeditions, led the Central Australian Exploring Expedition to Ayers Rock and the Olgas in 1889; he was followed by the Horn Expedition in 1896, and by a prospecting and geological party under the leadership of Herbert Basedow in 1903. These journeys were made by camel and subsequent visitors also used the same reliable means of transport. Despite the difficulties of travelling to Ayers Rock at the time, 24 names were recorded on the summit between 1930 and 1946. The track from the turn-off at Curtain Springs was graded in 1948 and the first official tour was conducted by Len Tuit in 1950.

Until the dedication of Uluru National Park in 1958, Ayers Rock and the Olgas were part of the Peterman Aboriginal Reserve, an area for which all whites were required to have an entry permit. The 126132-hectare park received more than 2000 visitors during the year after its creation. Bill Harney, the first ranger at Uluru, would travel with Len Tuit on the first tour of the season and then stay in the area during the winter and spring. Eddie Connellan, who had helped prepare the airstrip and who assisted in tour organisation, made the first official landing in April 1958. Scenic flights are now a regular feature of Uluru National Park.

The intention of most visitors, perhaps even an ambition in life, is to climb Ayers Rock. With an ascent of 1.6 kilometres and grades reaching 40 per cent, the climb

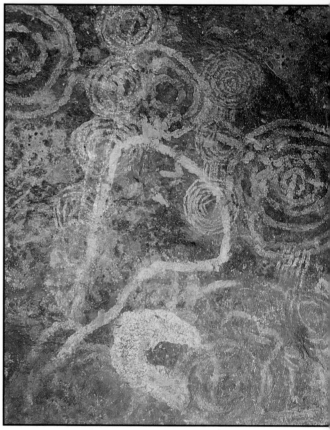

Top: The "Brain" is a collection of caves and depressions high up on the northern side of Ayers Rock. To the Aborigines it is Ngoru, the symbolic camp of the elders of Dreamtime.

Bottom: Red and yellow ochre, white ash and charcoal were used by the Aboriginals to compose symbolic drawings in well-sheltered caves around the base of Ayers Rock.

Top: One of the caves on the western side of Ayers Rock is illuminated by the late afternoon sunlight.

Bottom: A scenic flight over Ayers Rock, especially in the pictorial light of early morning or late afternoon, is one of Central Australia's most memorable experiences.

The many moods of Ayers Rock: During the course of the day, under different weather conditions and from various distances Ayers Rock may exhibit many moods and colours. At night Ayers Rock is a black, brooding hulk, then viewed from the east at dawn it becomes mauve and transforms into a soft, brilliant red. Throughout the day a warm brown colour remains but late in the afternoon when seen from the west brown changes to orange and then at sunset to a fiery red. Within minutes the red fades successively to brown and mauve and finally Ayers rock reverts to a great silhouetted shape on the desert horizon.

Under clear skies there is little colour change between mid-morning and mid-afternoon but at sunrise and sunset colour shift is rapid and features are starkly defined.

is not to be taken casually. A chain fence has been positioned along awkward sections and a dotted white line at the top indicates the route to the summit cairn. Most people, sensibly taking their time, reach the cairn in about an hour. Several deaths have occurred on the rock and the climb should be treated with respect. In the middle of the tourist season it is not uncommon for 2000 people to be climbing the rock every day.

Ayers Rock has many moods. It is a mysterious black hulk in the evening, an almost luminous red at sunrise and sunset, a variety of colours through the day, and a shimmering metallic silver when sunlight strikes the surface immediately after rain. Many people assume that it glows brilliantly every morning and evening and are disappointed that such effects do not occur each day. Maximum brilliance of colour depends on climatic conditions, with heavy cloud above the rock and a clear western sky being the most favourable combination. Few visitors have the good fortune to see Ayers Rock after rain: innumerable waterfalls and the sparkle of sunlight on wet rock are grand sights and truly one of the red centre's great gifts.

The best way to gain an appreciation of Ayers Rock is to attend one of the ranger tours; local geography, early exploration, flora and fauna, and Aboriginal mythology are explained and questions willingly answered. Most visitors are intrigued by Aboriginal culture, especially as represented in the paintings around the rock, which are located in caves well protected from rain, sunlight, and wind. They were drawn with fingertips or crude twig brushes, using yellow and red ochres, white ash, and charcoal. Simple designs illustrate legends from the Aboriginal Dreamtime, the Tjukurapa, where the world and man had their origin. The legends tell of many creatures and events, the best-known being associated with windulka (wind seed men), mala (plains wallabies), and kunia (carpet snakes). The age of the paintings is not known and, regrettably, a means of preservation is yet to be discovered.

It is assumed that the first Aborigines came from south-east Asia and that they have lived in Australia for at least 40000 years. Throughout the generations, each individual has been linked to one or more of the Dreamtime ancestors and has been tutored in the law and ritual of his or her totemic ancestor. Knowledge has been handed down in song and legend. The Yankuntjatjara people are the traditional 'owners' of Uluru, while the Pitjantjatjara, more recent arrivals, were forced into the area by adverse conditions in the western desert. Now the two groups are interrelated.

Like other Aborigines, these people adapted successfully to their environment and exhibited a strong sense of conservation. Essentially nomadic hunters and

Top: Tracts of Desert Fringe Myrtle are commonly found growing in red, sandy terrain amongst spinifex.

Bottom: Grevillea Eristachya is a favourite plant amongst Aboriginal children because the flower is spiced with nectar.

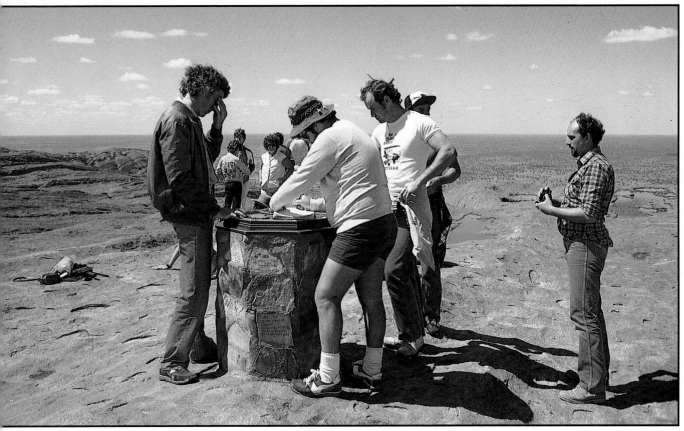

Top: Small children are no restriction to visitors who are determined to conquer the steep climb to the top of Ayers Rock.

Bottom: Visitors who reach the cairn at the top of Ayers Rock are invited to record their names in a special register.

Facing page: Depressions around the base of Ayers Rock fill with water after heavy rain and often create opportunities for unusual reflections.

Top: Kandju Gorge, located on the western side of Ayers Rock, is a picturesque place, especially when the waterhole is full.

Bottom: When rain falls, Maggie Springs, virtually a permanent natural reservoir, receives torrents of water from the vast surface area of Ayers Rock.

gatherers, they observed the habits of animals, determined the food and medicinal values of various plants and herbs and, most important of all, located waterholes and soaks or gleaned moisture from plants like the parakeelya and portulacas, certain desert trees, and even from water-retaining species of frogs.

Simple tools, artifacts and weapons were made from available materials: stones could grind seeds and crush fruits and be shaped as scrapers and knives. A type of vine growing in the Olgas was straightened to become spear shafts; boomerangs and spear throwers were manufactured from mulga trees, and carrying bowls were shaped from bean trees. Spear barbs were lashed on with animal sinew, while tendons and spinifex were used to make an adhesive. Kangaroos, wallabies, euros, dingoes, echidnas, possums, reptiles, and birds are a prime source of protein and at the same time provide skins, hair, feathers, bones, and tendons for a variety of uses. Insects, particularly the witchetty grub, also have great food value; seeds, yams, and certain roots are collected, along with native plums, rock figs and quandongs. Nectar can be extracted from grevillea plants, and honey from native bees and honey ants.

The aborigines have survived because they have lived harmoniously in their environment and placed greater emphasis on group, rather than individual, needs. There is much to be learnt from them. To see their paintings, hear their legends, learn of their culture, and just to be in their homeland, are vital parts of the Uluru experience.

Above: Cold, crisp mornings are no restriction to the experience of seeing the vibrant dawn colours of Ayers Rock.

Alice Springs

Alice Springs

Many people are surprised, if not disappointed, when they arrive in Alice Springs. Perhaps they expect to find a small frontier town with hitching rails and the occasional horse-drawn carriage. But 'the Alice' is a modern community, focal point for extensive pastoral and transport activities. There is a large industrial zone to the west, the population has reached 20000, and some 200000 visitors arrive each year.

The best months to be in Alice Springs, and indeed the whole of Central Australia, are August and September. Daytime temperatures are agreeable and the evenings have shed their chilly winter grip. Wildflowers add colour to the countryside and Alice Springs celebrates its most famous festivals: the Apex Rodeo and the Henley-on-Todd Regatta, usually spaced a week apart, are the principal highlights. The Rodeo occupies a full weekend and attracts nationwide competition. Bareback riding, saddle bronc, calf roping, bull riding, and steer wrestling are the standard events, supported by comedy and novelty routines. There is always plenty of action, clouds of dust, and light-hearted humour.

When it comes to humour, an essential outback characteristic, few events could match the hilarity of the Henley-on-Todd Regatta. A group of Rotarians devised the nonsense in 1962 as a once-only affair but the very dry joke proved to be such a success, raising money for local charities and providing some imaginative entertainment, that it was retained as an annual event and now attracts up to 10000 people. A section of dry river bed near the northern end of the town is set aside each year, and temporary fences and stands are erected. All the events, chaotic as they may appear, are in fact well organised. Strict rules are enforced to ensure fair play. For example, in boat races craft must travel bow-first and complete the 200-metre course with a full crew. Many other events, including surf-rescue, surf ski, sand shovelling, beauty contest, greasy mast, and a special 'Australia Cup' challenge between a local crew and Americans from the Pine Gap space research base, add variety to the afternoon's mayhem. At the end of the day motorised 'warships' compete in a demolition sea battle.

Alice Springs had its beginnings with the discovery of a permanent spring and the subsequent establishment of the Overland Telegraph Line. After John McDouall Stuart's expeditions of 1860 and 1861 opened up Central Australia, an overland telegraph linking the southern states of Australia with the rest of the world became a possibility. Charles Heavitree Todd, Superintendent of Telegraphs for South Australia, was allocated the task of supervising the construction of 3200 kilometres of line between Port Augusta and Darwin.

The passage forged by Stuart through the MacDonnell Ranges was deemed impractical for the

Top: The Royal Flying Doctor Service in Alice Springs administers medical services and general radio communications to remote areas of Central Australia.

Bottom: There is always plenty of action at the Apex Rodeo, one of the major springtime attractions in Alice Springs.

Previous page: The Alice Springs Telegraph Station was one of 12 constructed in the early 1870's for the Overland Telegraph Line between Adelaide and Darwin.

70

Top: The township of Alice Springs, looking south from Anzac Hill towards Mt. Undoolya, Heavitree Gap and Mt. Gillen.

Bottom: The American "crew" from the Pine Gap Base charges to the finish line in the America's Cup event at the Henley-on-Todd regatta.

telegraph and another alternative was sought. An advance exploration party led by John Ross passed through Heavitree Gap in March 1871. He met up with surveyor William Whitfield Mills, who had discovered a waterhole and dry river bed well suited to the route of the telegraph just a few kilometres north of the gap. The spring was named 'Alice' after Todd's wife, and his own names were used for the river and gap.

On 22 August 1872 the Overland Telegraph was completed. The Central Australian section of the line not only provided communication for Australia but also proved to be a convenient marker for explorations carried out by Ernest Giles, William Christie Gosse, Colonel Warburton, and H.V. Barclay.

Pastoral leases were released in Central Australia in 1872 and, by 1890, 14 leases were occupied and running more than 275000 head of cattle, sheep, and horses. Mineral wealth was also responsible for a great deal of Australia's early development and the events in Central Australia were no exception. The 1887 discovery of 'rubies' and then gold in the East MacDonnell Ranges attracted many prospectors. The Alice Springs telegraph station could not support the additional numbers of people and a nearby town, to be called Stuart, was gazetted on 29 November 1888. This frontier settlement had nine buildings in 1901 and was on the brink of failure until reef gold was discovered in the MacDonnells in 1902.

When the administration of the Northern Territory was transferred to the Commonwealth Government in 1911 it was agreed that the Commonwealth would purchase the Port Augusta-Oodnadatta railway in South Australia and extend the line to Stuart. The 'Ghan' railhead was completed in 1929, thus ensuring the future prospects of the town. In 1932 postal facilities were transferred into the town and the name officially changed to Alice Springs. During the Second World War many new facilities were established in 'the Alice' to service 5000 soldiers, and a sealed road was hastily constructed to provide a reliable connection with Darwin.

After the war, enterprising people began to realise the tourist potential of Central Australia and the location of Alice Springs as a convenient base. Facilities were built and tours organised to accommodate the start of a world-wide fascination for the unique features of Australia's red centre. The Alice Springs Telegraph Station National Park was gazetted in 1963 and is by far the most popular attraction in Alice Springs. Other regular attractions include the Flying Doctor Service, School of the Air, Casino, Emily Gap Camel Farm, and various museums, galleries and historic buildings.

Top: A brief ride on a camel or a safari into the desert can be arranged at Emily Gap Camel Farm.

Bottom: The Aboriginal heads and figures created by William Ricketts are part of the Pitchie Ritchie Wildlife Sanctuary.

Top: The Alice Springs Telegraph Station Historic Reserve contains faithfully restored stone buildings from the first European settlement in Central Australia.

Bottom: The highlight of Guth Gallery, one of the major attractions in Alice Springs, is a 360 degree painting panorama depicting all the famous landmarks of Central Australia.

The Devils Marbles

The Devils Marbles

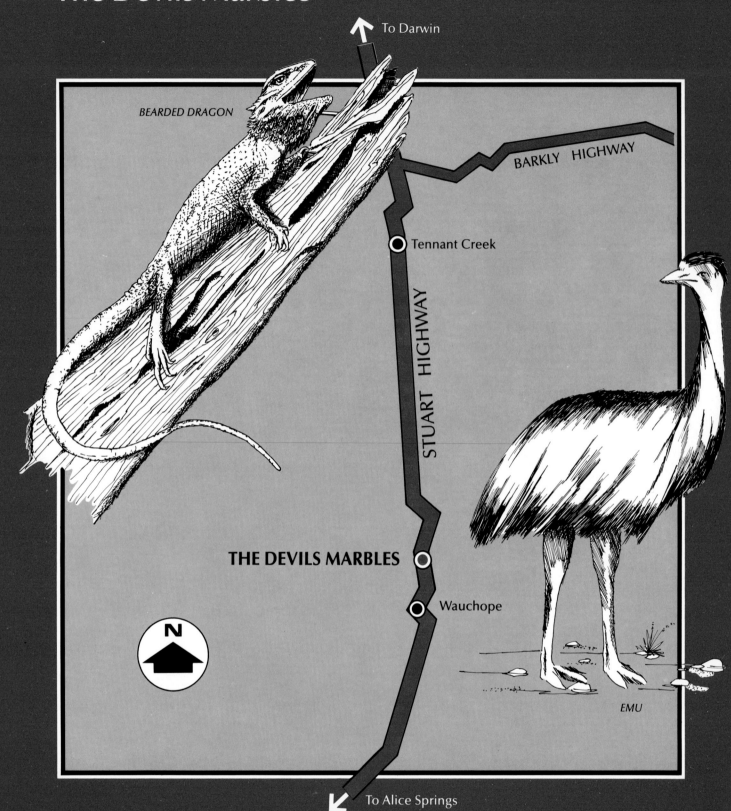

To Darwin

BEARDED DRAGON

BARKLY   HIGHWAY

Tennant Creek

STUART   HIGHWAY

N

THE DEVILS MARBLES

Wauchope

EMU

To Alice Springs

Previous page: A group of Devil's Marbles lie curiously stacked on the side of the Stuart Highway between Alice Springs and Tennant Creek. Aboriginals consider the boulders to be giant eggs laid by the sacred rainbow serpent.

Facing page: Some of the boulders in the Devil's Marbles assume eerie shapes.

The Devils Marbles

Geographically, the Devils Marbles are part of Central Australia but, because they lie 393 kilometres north of Alice Springs, they cannot be conveniently linked with other places of particular interest. For this reason they are generally seen only by people travelling on the Stuart Highway between Alice Springs and Tennant Creek.

Much of Australia's outback scenery gains impact from its unexpectedness: there is little to break the seemingly endless horizon of semi-desert along the Stuart Highway north of Alice Springs, but about 100 kilometres south of Tennant Creek the landscape suddenly changes and large boulders appear scattered or stacked on both sides of the road.

Some of the marbles have a diameter of as much as 6 metres, but they appear even larger. They were once part of a single granite mass composed of three main sets of joint planes at right angles to each other. Splits along lines of weakness eventually broke the granite into large, rectangular blocks. Erosion weathered the blocks, to form rounded shapes, piled upon each other or delicately poised. Long hot days followed by cold nights caused repeated expansion and contraction of the rock, resulting in the cracking and peeling off of surface layers.

Strewn across a wide, shallow valley, like the discarded toys of a giant, the Devils Marbles are now part of a 1828-hectare conservation reserve. In the midst of a harsh, arid environment the boulders provide a cool, sheltered refuge for plants and animals. Pygmy spiny-tailed goannas inhabit rock crevices, while larger sand goannas prefer the thick clumps of spinifex between the boulders. Finches are relatively common and bottle swallows build mud nests under rock overhangs. A scattering of trees adds a touch of softness to the boulders, and stately ghost gums, seeking out their preferred habitat, are often wedged in rock fissures. All trees play an important role in the ecology of the region: even decayed, fallen branches provide an invaluable link in the food chain for indigenous birds and reptiles. Visitors are requested not to collect firewood in the reserve.

The Devil's Marbles are best viewed in the soft, warm light of dawn or dusk, when the brown and red shades of the boulders are accentuated. The flat tones created by the harsh midday sun certainly are uninspiring compared to the rich colours of early morning and late afternoon.

Above: The Devil's Marbles are contained within a 1828 hectare conservation reserve 393 kilometres north of Alice Springs. The boulders were originally part of a single granite mass which broke up along lines of weakness. Large daily temperature variations cause the rock surface to expand and contract and eventually peel away. This process of exfoliation, combined with the erosive forces of wind and water, have rounded off rock surfaces and left many boulders strangely detached or closely piled together.
The Devil's Marbles are fascinating to explore, particularly in the warm light of early morning or late afternoon.

Henbury Meteorite
Craters National Park

Henbury Meteorite Craters National Park

Henbury Meteorite Craters Conservation Reserve occupies 17 hectares and is located 147 kilometres south-west of Alice Springs. The reserve contains 13 craters, all formed by the impact of fragments emanating from a single meteor. The largest crater is 180 metres long, 6 metres above ground level and 15 metres deep, while the smallest is a barely recognisable 6 metres long and a few centimetres deep. Several of the craters have unusual drainage patterns and plants; they are wildlife refuges in a harsh desert environment.

An Aboriginal name for the area, 'sun walk fire devil rock', suggests that Aborigines witnessed the fall of the meteorite, estimated to have occurred about 4700 years ago. The site was not discovered until the 1920s, but it has since proved to be of considerable scientific interest. It was used by the United States National Aeronautic and Space Administration (NASA) as a familiarisation location for the manned moon missions and has contributed to an understanding of formations on other planets. Over 500 kilograms of meteorite fragments, composed primarily of iron and a small percentage of nickel, have been collected, the biggest piece weighing about 100 kilograms. Some pieces have become doorstops in Central Australian homes, and gem and souvenir hunters have generally denuded the immediate area of specimens.

Although the Henbury Craters are not spectacular in comparison to the famous landmarks of Central Australia, they possess a measure of curiosity which makes the short detour from the main road a worthwhile venture.

Chambers Pillar

Chambers Pillar

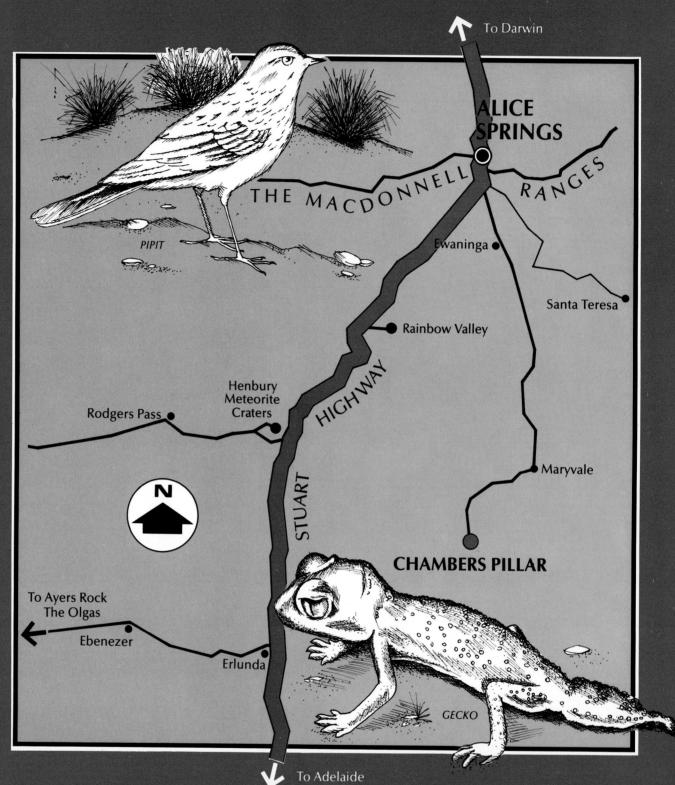

To Darwin

ALICE SPRINGS

THE MACDONNELL RANGES

Ewaninga

Santa Teresa

Rainbow Valley

Henbury Meteorite Craters

Rodgers Pass

STUART HIGHWAY

Maryvale

CHAMBERS PILLAR

To Ayers Rock The Olgas

Ebenezer

Erlunda

GECKO

To Adelaide

PIPIT

Previous page: In 1860 John McDouall Stuart was the first European to reach Chambers Pillar. He described the structure as being a "locomotive engine with a funnel".

Facing page: Chambers Pillar Historic Reserve is not a major tourist attraction in Central Australia, primarily because access is restricted to four wheel drive vehicles.

Chambers Pillar

'Nothing so much as a number of old castles in ruins.'

Explorer John McDouall Stuart

Relative isolation and difficult access have meant that Chambers Pillar and its associated totem-like structures are not well known. The 340-hectare Chambers Pillar Historic Reserve lies 160 kilometres south of Alice Springs and is usually approached through Maryvale Station. Conventional vehicle access ends at Hugh River, 5 kilometres past Maryvale, and thereafter steep, stony inclines and a series of sandhills necessitate the use of four-wheel-drive vehicles.

Chambers Pillar, centrepiece of the reserve, stands 50 metres above the surrounding plain; it is about 18 metres long at the top and about 6 metres wide. This dramatic landmark is the remnant of a mesa or butte in the final stages of decay and is a breakaway from the nearby Charlotte Range. The gently sloping mound of the 'pedestal' on which the pillar stands is covered by loose sandstone talus which has fallen from the pillar.

The existing rock structures are vestiges of an ancient plateau formed of sandstone deposits which were laid down about 350 million years ago. Wind and rain have eroded the softer, pebbly sandstone and gradually lowered the surrounding plain.

Venturing north in his first attempt to cross Australia in April 1860, John McDouall Stuart became the first European to record contact with Chambers Pillar. He described the structure as 'a locomotive engine with a funnel' and named it after James Chambers who, with William Finke, had financed his expedition.

John Ross, returning from his task of investigating a route for the proposed Overland Telegraph Line, visited the area on 22 September 1870, and was followed by Ernest Giles two years later. Giles, one of Australia's most determined explorers, was noted for his poetic impressions. In his book *Australia Twice Traversed* he recalls his encounter with Chambers Pillar.

'It's outline was most imposing. Upon reaching it, I found it to be a columnar structure, standing upon a pedestal, which is perhaps eighty feet high, and composed of loose white sandstone, having vast numbers of large blocks lying about in all directions. From the centre of the pedestal rises the pillar, composed also of the same kind of rock; at its top, and for some twenty to thirty feet from its summit, the column itself must be seventy to eighty feet above the pedestal. It is split at the top into two points. There it stands, a vast monument of geological periods that must have elapsed since the mountain ridge of which it was formerly a part was washed by the action of old man's waves into mere sandhills at its feet.'

Above: Chambers Pillar is the remnant of a mesa in the final stages of decay. The imposing natural monument stands on a pedestal covered by loose sandstone talus.

Chambers Pillar

Until the advent of the railway in the 1920s, Chambers Pillar had been a convenient desert landmark for journeys between Adelaide and Alice Springs. Many of the early explorers, pioneer pastoralists, and Overland Telegraph employees climbed to the base of the pillar and inscribed their names or initials in the soft, white sandstone. Some engravings record a date as early as 1853 but these are possibly the work of more recent visitors who have defaced the pillar. One inscription commences with the letters 'GI' but the remainder has since broken away. This was perhaps the hand of Giles as he recorded:

'The stone is so friable that names can be cut in it to almost any depth with a pocket-knife; so loose, indeed, is it, that one almost feels alarmed lest it should fall while one is scratching at its base.'

Chambers Pillar has its place in Aboriginal mythology. In the dreamtime, the gecko ancestor *Itirkawara* left the Finke River and journeyed north-east to his birthplace. As he travelled, he became a powerful superhuman and developed a violent temper. He slew several of his ancestors with a stone knife and, flushed with the success of his deeds, disregarded strict marriage codes by taking a wife from the wrong kinship group. Both he and the unfortunate girl were banished and forced to retreat into the desert, where they eventually perished. Itirkawara turned into the pillar and the girl became the low hill, about 500 metres to the north-east, which is now known as Castle Rock. The knob-tailed geckos, descendants of Itirkawara, are fairly common in the area.

The Historic Reserve which encloses Chambers Pillar was declared in 1970. Casuarina trees, better known as desert oaks, stand among red sand dunes and grassy flats in the immediate area. The Conservation Commission of the Northern Territory has prepared several tracks and established picnic areas and camp sites. There is no water and firewood is scarce. Ranger patrols are made on a regular basis.

Like all the great rock monuments in central Australia, Chambers Pillar, the Castle Rock, and other features are best viewed at sunrise or sunset, when colours assume their greatest intensity. Upon leaving the area, the visitor will surely agree with Ernest Giles:

'We turned our backs on this peculiar monument, and left it in its loneliness and its grandeur — "clothed in white sandstone, mystical, wonderful!"'

Above: According to Aboriginal mythology Castle Rock is the remains of a native girl who was abducted by Itirkawara, a powerful super-human who murdered several of his family group.

90

Above: A towering rock structure in Chambers Pillar
Historic Reserve has eroded in such a way as to leave
two large rocks tightly wedged between supports.

Gosse Bluff

Gosse Bluff

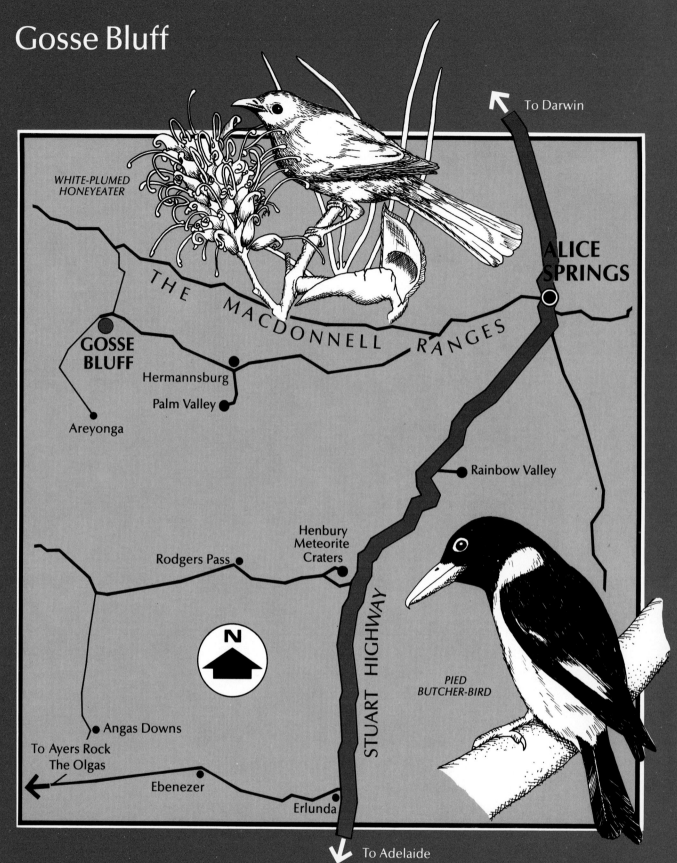

WHITE-PLUMED HONEYEATER

To Darwin

THE MACDONNELL RANGES

ALICE SPRINGS

GOSSE BLUFF

Hermannsburg

Palm Valley

Areyonga

Rainbow Valley

Henbury Meteorite Craters

Rodgers Pass

N

STUART HIGHWAY

PIED BUTCHER-BIRD

Angas Downs

To Ayers Rock The Olgas

Ebenezer

Erlunda

To Adelaide

Previous page: Early morning sunlight streams across the western side of Gosse Bluff outlining caverns and outcrops on the steep slopes and the clumps of spinifex which can make any climb awkward.

Facing page: The peaks of Gosse Bluff not only afford a better appreciation of the encirclement of mountains but also distant views of the MacDonnell Ranges.

Gosse Bluff

The unmistakable shape of Gosse Bluff is seen on Missionary Plain, south of the West MacDonnell Ranges. The large, circular range of mountains encloses a pound, but the circular shape of the formation is not apparent from the surrounding plain and this, no doubt, accounts for the 'Bluff' misnomer.

Although Gosse Bluff was discovered more than a century ago, its geological history has only recently been determined by geological and geophysical surveys and regional mapping. Several theories were discounted, including that of a fossil mud volcano or a massive volcanic eruption. The formation is attributed to the impact of a comet some 130 million years ago. Lack of debris in the immediate area lends support to the theory that the comet was composed of ice and frozen gases which evaporated upon impact. The detonation was probably equivalent to a force 200 times greater than the Hiroshima bomb and the effects of the impact would have been experienced worldwide.

Such a great impact would have required a comet speed of around 70 kilometres per second. Before vaporisation, the comet penetrated about 600 metres below ground level, causing a rock strata breakage more than 4 kilometres deep. The shock wave compressed the rock and set off an immediate rebound which formed a crater about 25 kilometres in diameter and forced a highly resistant core of rock layers to the surface. These rocks are now the bluff. Erosion over millions of years has removed the outer rim and the crater has filled with sediment.

The mountainous crater rim was discovered in 1872 by Ernest Giles, who named it after his friend Harry Gosse, one of the officers at the Alice Springs Telegraph Station, and not after the explorer William Christie Gosse. Giles mapped the eastern walls and, searching for water, rode into the interior via 'a small creek, lined with gum trees' on the north-eastern side. Little water was found so Giles elected not to explore the area in detail, preferring to continue west along the MacDonnell Ranges where waterholes were more reliable.

Today the creek bed provides the only vehicular access to the pound. The interior is generally flat and sparsely covered with spinifex; it has an average diameter of 2.5 kilometres. The mountains rise to about 200 metres above the plain and contain rock overhangs and small caverns. Most peaks can be scaled in 15-20 minutes and they provide panoramic views of the pound and the distant MacDonnell Ranges.

Gosse Bluff is now a scientific reserve. There are no facilities for visitors and no reliable supplies of water. Seismic tracks intersect the original route leading to the entrance to the bluff. Conventional vehicles may enter the pound but loose sand on the track makes four-wheel-drive transport more reliable.

Top: The steep slopes and ridges of Gosse Bluff are dotted with rock overhangs and caverns.

Bottom: Plants in Central Australia manage to grow in sandy soils and in unlikely places, like this Helichrysum clinging to a small ledge at the top of Gosse Bluff.

Above: Various species of Xanthorrhoea, commonly known as Grass Trees, Blackboys or Yacca gums, are spread throughout Australia. In the desert of Central Australia the spear-like flower spike, grass like leaf "skirt" and sturdy black trunk make the blackboy easy to identify. The plant is remarkably resistant to fire and insect attack and can survive for centuries.

Hermannsburg Mission and Palm Valley

Hermannsburg Mission and Palm Valley

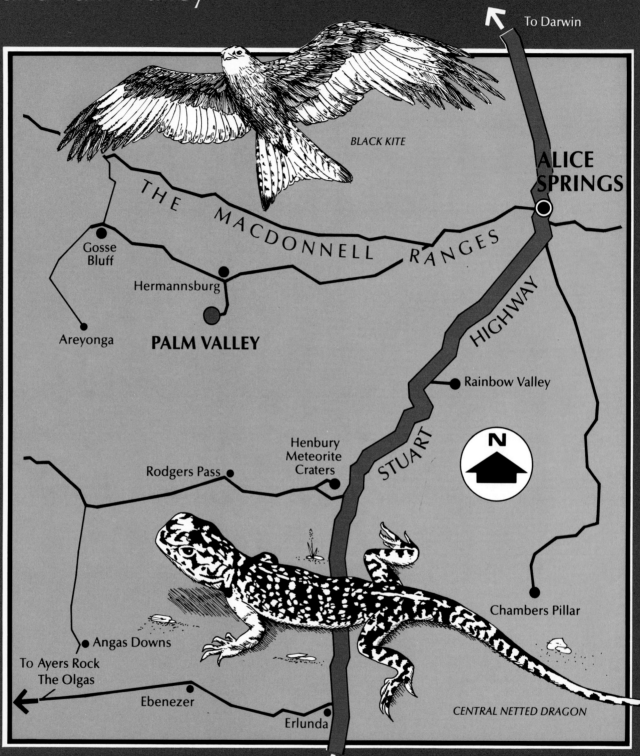

BLACK KITE

To Darwin

ALICE SPRINGS

THE MACDONNELL RANGES

Gosse Bluff

Hermannsburg

PALM VALLEY

Areyonga

Rainbow Valley

STUART HIGHWAY

N

Henbury Meteorite Craters

Rodgers Pass

Chambers Pillar

Angas Downs

To Ayers Rock The Olgas

Ebenezer

Erlunda

To Adelaide

CENTRAL NETTED DRAGON

Previous page: The cabbage palms (Livistona Mariae) in Palm Valley are descendants of trees which once surrounded an inland sea.

Facing page: Encrustation ring patterns are formed around shallow ponds in Palm Valley as water gradually evaporates.

Hermannsburg Mission and Palm Valley

Hermannsburg Mission lies on the northern bank of the Finke River, 136 kilometres west of Alice Springs. A Lutheran Mission was established there in 1877 following an initial allocation of 200 square miles by the Commissioner of Crown Lands. The first dwellings were made from timber and grass, and a stone church-school was built in 1880. The first Superintendent of the settlement, Pastor A.M. Kempe, produced an Aranda-language dictionary and his successor, Pastor C.T.F. Strethlow, translated the New Testament into Aranda and supervised the 1897 construction of the church-school house which still stands today.

The most famous name associated with the Hermannsburg Mission is Albert Namatjira, the Aborigine whose paintings so brilliantly captured the colour and magnificence of Central Australia. In the 1930s Namatjira became one of the first Aboriginal artists of the Aranda School to adopt the Western style of perspective.

Despite many problems, the mission survives and it is now part of a cattle station manned by Aboriginal labour. In order to protect the privacy of the Aborigines and to avoid interference in the functions of the mission, large-scale tourism has not been encouraged. However, visitors are made welcome and may purchase fuel and supplies. An entry permit to Hermannsburg Mission is not required.

The turn-off to Finke Gorge National Park and Palm Valley lies just beyond Hermannsburg and across the Finke River. The track follows 16 kilometres of normally dry river bed. The route is not suitable for conventional vehicles. Ernest Giles discovered the southern opening of the Finke River Gorge and entered the 'Glen', as he called it, on 30 August 1872. Seven days later he passed through the northern side. The discovery and naming of Palm Valley, a side gorge branching west from the Finke River, are attributed to one of the first Hermannsburg missionaries. The name was conveniently borrowed from Giles' 'Glen of Palms', an area lying at the southern end of the Finke Gorge and now known as Boggy Hole.

Established in 1967, the Finke Gorge National Park occupies 45900 hectares and incorporates part of the Finke River (believed to be the world's oldest river), Palm Valley, and a vast area of sand dunes to the south. The most remarkable features of the area are its primeval character, the presence of some of the world's oldest plant species, and minimal evidence of human intrusion.

The large semi-circular valley known as the Amphitheatre has several distinctive red sandstone features which have been given names like Battleship, Sundial, Cathedral, and Popeye. Initiation Rock, an elevated rock outcrop where youths from the Aranda tribe took part in ceremonial rituals, is an accessible vantage point from which the entire Amphitheatre can be seen.

Top: The old school house at Hermannsburg Mission, built in 1897, still stands today.

Bottom: Initiation Rock, a site where young Aboriginals of the Aranda tribe were involved in rituals, stands on an elevated position overlooking the Amphitheatre.

Top: Late afternoon light highlights one of the massive rock features in the Amphitheatre of Finke Gorge National Park.

Bottom: The extent of the luxuriant growth in Palm Valley is best seen from a high vantage point.

Hermannsburg Mission
and Palm Valley

Palm Creek and Cycad Gorge mark the entrance to Palm Valley. Towering rock walls, dotted with small cycad palms and ferns, lead to an area where cabbage palms are concentrated. These trees, some 3000 in number, are descendants of palms which surrounded the shores of an inland sea millions of years ago. They grow quickly to a height of 14-20 metres, and reach full maturity in 150-300 years. The palms and about 30 of the 300 plant species in the area are now regarded as being some of the rarest in the world. Bamboo patches, ghost gums and native pines are scattered about: a most unlikely assortment, especially in the middle of an arid region.

Above: Sundial Rock and Popeye are two distinctive features to be found in the vast Amphitheatre of Finke Gorge National Park.

ottom left: River red gums and native pines mingle th cabbage palms in a unique Australian oasis.

ottom right: A tall, graceful palm, with leaf fronds nging to its base, is isolated on rocky terrain in Palm alley.

Kings Canyon

Kings Canyon

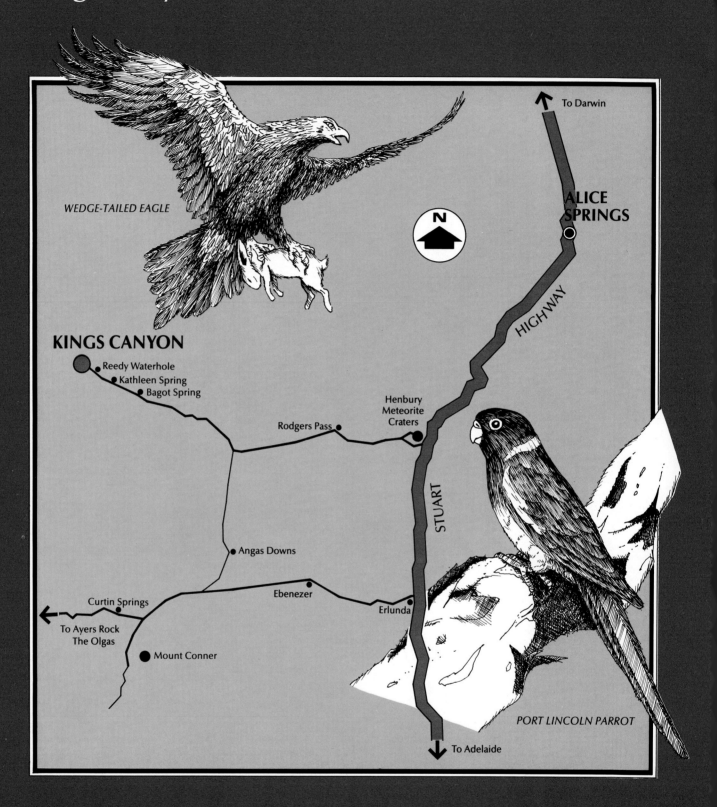

WEDGE-TAILED EAGLE

KINGS CANYON

• Reedy Waterhole
• Kathleen Spring
• Bagot Spring

Rodgers Pass •

Henbury
Meteorite
Craters

To Darwin

ALICE
SPRINGS

HIGHWAY

STUART

• Angas Downs

Ebenezer

Erlunda

Curtin Springs

To Ayers Rock
The Olgas

• Mount Conner

To Adelaide

PORT LINCOLN PARROT

Previous page: It is not difficult to understand why the weathered dome-shaped buttresses at the top of Kings Canyon have been described as ancient ruins from a "Lost City".

Facing page: Kings Canyon country can be inviting to explore but the terrain can be extremely difficult to negotiate.

Kings Canyon

Kings Canyon, the most spectacular gorge in Central Australia, lies at the western end of the George Gill Range, some 320 kilometres south-east of Alice Springs. Most visitors arrive at Kings Canyon from Wallara Tourist Ranch (where accommodation and facilities are available) or, using four-wheel-drive vehicles, from the west through Aboriginal land. A permit, obtainable from the Central Land Council, is required to cross this land, and indeed any Aboriginal reserve in Central Australia.

The watercourse from Kings Canyon was discovered by Ernest Giles during his 1872 expedition. He bestowed the name Kings Creek after Fieldon King, one of his financiers, and allocated names to other prominent landmarks in the area, including Carmichael Crag and the waterholes Penny, Reedy, Stoke, and Bagot. The popular Reedy waterhole 15 kilometres to the east of Kings Canyon, is, according to Giles' description, actually part of a stream he called 'Penny'.

Concerned about Aboriginal attacks, Giles did not venture into Kings Canyon itself, nor did William Christie Gosse, who passed through the same area in 1873. During the late 1870s, Giles did apply for a rent-free lease over almost 5000 square kilometres of Kings Canyon country, which he hoped would be granted in recognition of his explorations in the area. The government agreed that Giles was entitled to first claim but, because the lease was not offered free and he could not afford stock, Giles forfeited the opportunity. Had he proceeded, he certainly would have discovered the canyon and the fascinating features above it.

Graziers moved into the area in the early 1900s, forcing Aborigines out of the sacred canyon they called Watarka (after the acacia trees there). The canyon remained deserted for half a century until Jack Cotterill, his son Jim, and Arthur Liddle, owner of Angus Downs, ventured into the area. Realising the tourist potential of Kings Canyon, the Cotterills purchased a small lease from Angus Downs, constructed buildings at Wallara and forged 100 kilometres of track to the canyon. The original track has since become a broad gravel road and is currently maintained by the Northern Territory Department of Transport and Works.

The entrance to Kings Canyon is wide, has a moderate coverage of vegetation and is flanked by steep slopes. After about 2 kilometres' penetration into the ranges, the valley turns eastward and becomes a long canyon with vertical sides towering over 200 metres high. The vast, smooth face of the southern wall is the result of huge rock slabs breaking away evenly along vertical joint lines.

A walk along the canyon floor takes the hiker past lofty river red gums, isolated pools of water, and boulders which increase rapidly in size as the head of the canyon

Top: The trek from the floor of Kings Canyon, through the "Lost City" and "Garden of Eden" culminates in an excellent vantage point at the head of the canyon.

Bottom: The smooth southern face of Kings Canyon is the result of large rock slabs shearing off evenly along vertical joint lines.

Top: The landscape above Kings Canyon is an extensive array of terraces, crevices and valleys set amongst heavily eroded horizontal sandstone layers.

Bottom: Nature has created some remarkable shapes in the Kings Canyon landscape.

Kings Canyon

is approached. But the most interesting walk starts from the end of the vehicular track, follows a steep climb to a point overlooking the canyon, and then proceeds into the Lost City, an extensive area of rock domes and terraces reminiscent of ruins from an ancient civilisation. Over millions of years the elements have eroded horizontal sandstone layers, leaving a remarkable landscape.

In the Lost City, small crevices quickly become narrow chasms 20 metres deep, which run almost parallel and join a steep-walled valley leading to a waterfall at the head of Kings Canyon. The valley, known as the Garden of Eden, contains a series of deep, dark pools and lush vegetation — a remarkable sight in the midst of a great arid region.

Most visitors spend only a day in Kings Canyon. In that time, they see the main attractions but, to really absorb the beauty of the immediate and adjacent areas, several days are necessary. At present there are no facilities at Kings Canyon, and no drinking water. The entire area is destined to be declared a national park, an action that will ensure adequate environmental protection and provide some basic amenities.

Top: One of the impressive domes in the "Lost City" assumes an almost luminous glow in the light of the setting sun.

Bottom: A ray of light catches one of the varieties of Helichrysum, a plant commonly found in high, rocky places.

Top: The domes and terraces above Kings Canyon are cut by narrow crevices, some as deep as 30 metres.

Bottom: The "Garden of Eden" is a narrow valley system above Kings Canyon. Permanent waterholes support lush growth, including the rare cycad Macrozamia Macdonnellii.

Facing page: Bagot Spring is situated between Kings Canyon and Wallara Tourist Ranch and is one of several water sources discovered by Ernest Giles.

Top: Desert Oak Drive, located south of Wallara, contains many fine specimens of this attractive tree. Curiously the young oaks, known as Pencil Pines, bear little resemblance to the adult tree.

Bottom: Reedy Waterhole can be a refreshing place to linger after a hot day's travel but swimmers will find the waters to be very cold.

Mount Conner

Mount Conner

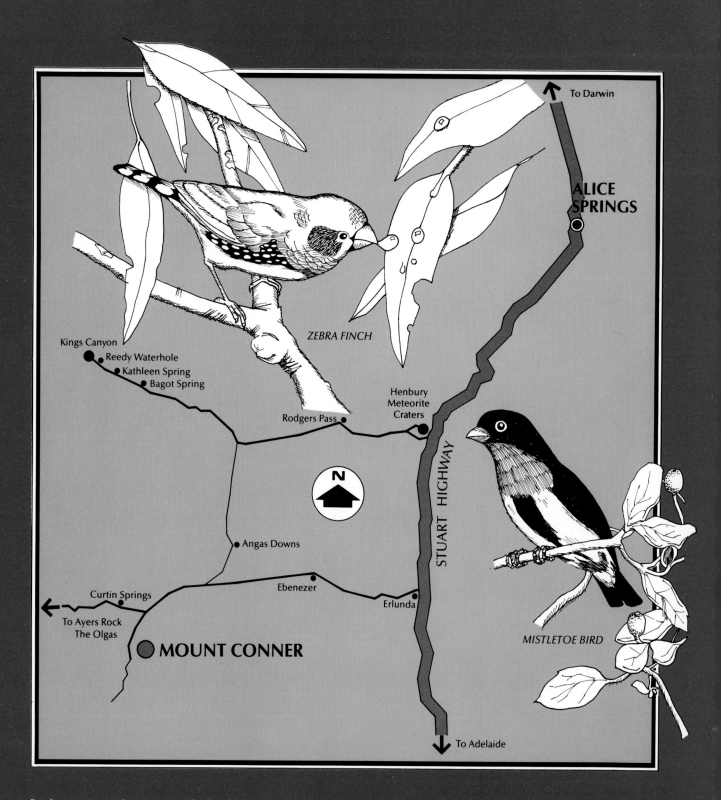

ZEBRA FINCH

Kings Canyon
Reedy Waterhole
Kathleen Spring
Bagot Spring

Rodgers Pass

Henbury
Meteorite
Craters

To Darwin

ALICE SPRINGS

N

STUART HIGHWAY

Angas Downs

Ebenezer

Curtin Springs

Erlunda

To Ayers Rock
The Olgas

MOUNT CONNER

MISTLETOE BIRD

To Adelaide

Previous page: Mt. Conner, pictured a few kilometres south of Curtain Springs, is a horse-shoe shaped mesa with sheer vertical walls along the northern face.

Facing page: The plateau-like summit of Mt. Conner is covered with spinifex and mulga scrub and provides extensive panoramas of the desert.

Mount Conner

Mount Conner, a quartzite mesa, or table-topped mountain, lies south of the main road to Ayers Rock and the Olgas, and is often mistaken for Ayers Rock. It was discovered by William Christie Gosse in July 1873 and named after M.L. Conner, a South Australian politician. The Aborigines know the mountain as *Artila* and believe it to be the former home of the infamous *Ninya,* or Icemen. These ice-covered creatures created the cold winter nights by allowing ice to drop from their bodies and become ground frost. Legend tells that the deep cracks which form in the soles of the Aborigines' feet are caused by treading on ice left in the grass by the Ninya. The association of ice with a desert may seem a paradox but furrows in some coarse rocks indicate they were embedded in ice during a glacial period.

The semi-circular mountain is about 5 kilometres long and 2 kilometres wide, running east-west; it stands 244 metres above ground level. Apart from the southern side, which is intercepted by several gorges, the upper walls of Mount Conner are vertical for about 90 metres; the lower portions are steep and covered with talus. The Mount Conner rocks, considerably older then those of Ayers Rock and the Olgas, were deposited in an ancient sea bed about 1000 million years ago. At that time the present surface of the mountain was part of a vast plain. Erosion has lowered the plain and left this dominant hulk.

Mount Conner is part of Curtain Springs pastoral lease and is not part of central Australian tourist itineraries. To see the mountain at close quarters please seek permission and detailed directions from the Curtain Springs roadhouse. The access track passes the ruins of the old Mount Conner homestead, which stand on a ridge overlooking Aneri Well, some water tanks, stockyards, and a large claypan. Gorges on the southern side of Mount Conner can be scaled despite their steepness and sharp spinifex spikes. The view from the top is splendid: the Musgrave Ranges on the southern horizon, the George Gill Ranges to the north and, 85 kilometres to the west, the merging shapes of Ayers Rock and the Olgas. Wedge-tailed eagles are common around the summit and euros can be spotted from time to time.

Top: There are many sheltered caverns on the steep southern slopes of Mt. Conner.

Bottom: An almost conical shaped hill, covered with spinifex and capped with a rock outcrop, is part of the rugged terrain on the southern side of Mt. Conner.

Top: From a northern aspect Mt. Conner appears formidable but valleys on the southern side permit access to the top.

Bottom: The valleys on the southern side of Mt. Conner are distinguishable, even from the distant site of the old Mt. Conner station.

Rainbow Valley

Rainbow Valley

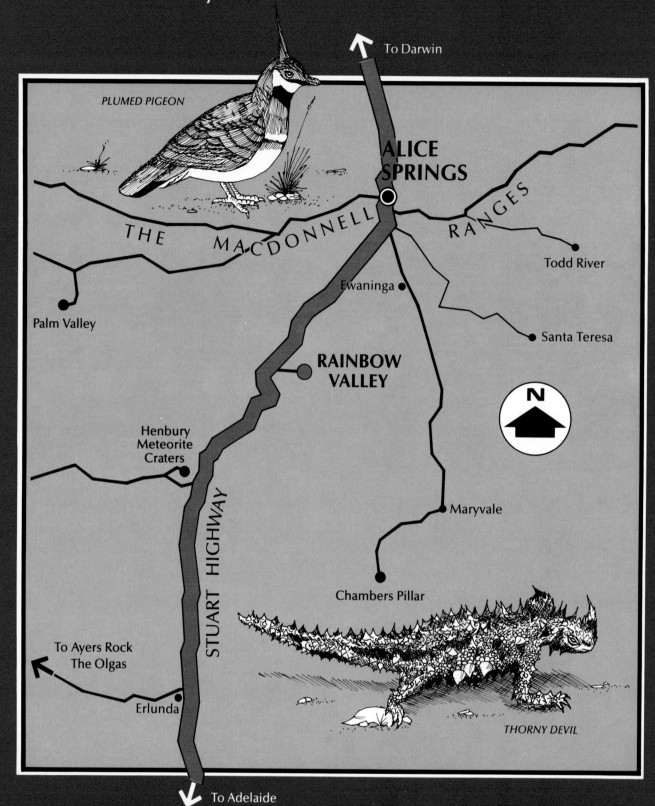

PLUMED PIGEON

THE MACDONNELL RANGES

ALICE SPRINGS

To Darwin

Todd River

Ewaninga

Santa Teresa

Palm Valley

N

RAINBOW VALLEY

Henbury
Meteorite
Craters

Maryvale

STUART HIGHWAY

To Ayers Rock
The Olgas

Chambers Pillar

Erlunda

THORNY DEVIL

To Adelaide

Previous page and facing page: The beautiful colours and bold outcrops of Rainbow Valley are accentuated by the warmth of the setting sun.

Above and facing page: Rainbow Valley is part of Orange Creek Station and is located about 120 kilometres south of Alice Springs. The area is scheduled to be declared a 30 square kilometre reserve and will be administered by the Conservation Commission of the Northern Territory.

Little is known about the Aboriginal significance of the area or of early European exploration, however continuing research may provide some details.

Rainbow Valley is part of the Hermannsburg sandstone category and as such is about 350 million years old. Joints, or stress fractures, which occurred during major earth movements, have shaped the dramatic rock outcrops. The fractures are mainly vertical and strike in an east-west direction, whereas the vertical faces on the northern side are exposed joint surfaces.

The presence of limonite (an iron oxide), occurring as a thin veneer over the component sand grains, gives the formations their characteristic warm colours. Generally the colours move from white at the base to deep red at the top. This is the result of laterisation, a process where underground iron oxide particles are dissolved by water and transported by capillary action to higher levels.

In its own inimitable way nature has produced some exquisite patterns and some unusual shapes in Rainbow Valley. The "Lion's Head" and "Mushroom Rock" are easily recognisable features.

Many famous landmarks in Central Australia assume their greatest impact in the light of early morning or late afternoon. The features of Rainbow Valley certainly are no exception.

Central Australia
Points of Interest.

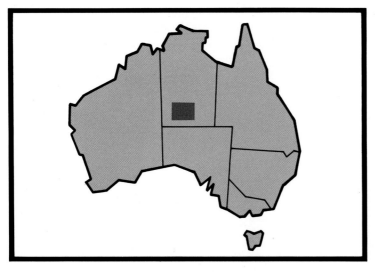

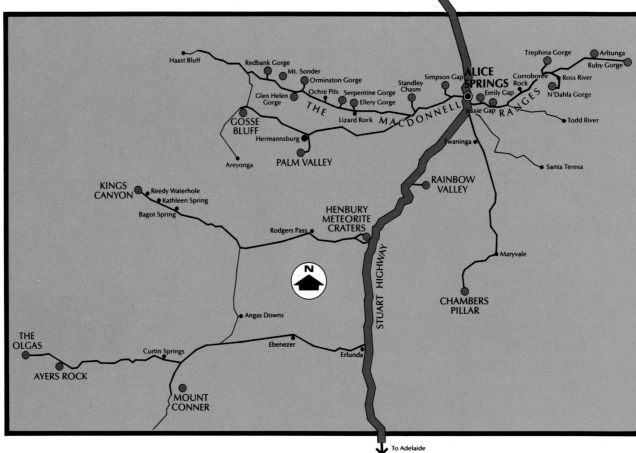

First published 1984 by Golden Press Pty Ltd
Incorporated in New South Wales
2-12 Tennyson Road, Gladesville, NSW 2111, Australia

© Trevern and Anna Dawes

Printed in Hong Kong by Dai Nippon Printing Co.
Designed by Philip Eldridge Design and Artwork (Sydney)
Typeset by Keyset Phototype Pty. Ltd. (Sydney) in 10/10pt Optima

National Library of Australia cataloguing-in-publication data.

Dawes, Trevern.
Central Australia through the lens.

ISBN O 85558 898 5.

1. Australia, Central — Description and travel —
Views. I. Dawes, Anna. II. Title.

919.42'0463